For the amazing Melinda Pavlata of Moody Street Circus. Without her assistance, this story would never have danced its way into the world.
—L.R.

For Peggy and Patty
—R.G.

Text copyright © 2020 by Lisa Robinson
Jacket art and interior illustrations copyright © 2020 by Rebecca Green

All rights reserved. Published in the United States by Schwartz & Wade Books, an imprint of Random House Children's Books, a division of Penguin Random House LLC, New York.

Schwartz & Wade Books and the colophon are trademarks of Penguin Random House LLC.

Visit us on the Web! rhcbooks.com
Educators and librarians, for a variety of teaching tools, visit us at RHTeachersLibrarians.com

Library of Congress Cataloging-in-Publication Data
Names: Robinson, Lisa, author. | Green, Rebecca, illustrator.
Title: Madame Saqui: revolutionary rope dancer / Lisa Robinson, Rebecca
Green [illustrator].
Description: First edition. | New York: Schwartz & Wade Books, 2020. | Audience: Age 4–8. | Audience: K to grade 3.
Identifiers: LCCN 2019007528 | ISBN 978-0-525-57997-7 (hardcover) | ISBN 978-0-525-57998-4 (hardcover library binding)
ISBN 978-0-525-57999-1 (ebook)
Subjects: LCSH: Saqui, Marguerite Antoinette Lalanne, 1786–1866—Juvenile literature.
Aerialists—France—Biography—Juvenile literature.
Classification: LCC GV550.2.S37 R63 2020 | DDC 796.46—dc23

The text of this book is set in Cochin.
The illustrations were rendered in gouache, colored pencil, and water-soluble crayon and edited digitally.
Book design by Rachael Cole

MANUFACTURED IN CHINA
10 9 8 7 6 5 4 3 2 1
First Edition

MADAME SAQUI

Revolutionary Rope Dancer

WRITTEN BY

LISA ROBINSON &

ILLUSTRATED BY

REBECCA GREEN

schwartz & wade books · new york

In 1791, in Paris, inside le Théâtre des Grands Danseurs du Roi, five-year-old Marguerite-Antoinette Lalannc was making her debut.

She flipped.

She tumbled.

She cartwheeled.

High above, her mother and father danced across a tightrope.

The crowd cheered.

Marguerite waved and bowed and vowed that one day

she would dance on a tightrope, too.

Meanwhile, outside,

French citizens were stirring up a revolution.

Angry with a king who had so much

when they had so little,

hordes of hungry people marched in the streets,

demanding lower prices for bread.

During these troubled times, Marguerite's parents
fed their family by working at the theater.
But one night, her father, Navarin the Great, fell
and broke his leg.
The famous rope dancer would never perform again.

Navarin insisted that the family find
a less dangerous way to earn a living.
And so, in September 1792,
as riots erupted through the city's streets,
the Lalannes fled to the countryside,
leaving Paris and their circus life behind.

For the next four years, in Caen and then in Tours,

Marguerite learned to fit and sell lace bonnets;

her father and her older brother, Laurent, peddled potions and pulled teeth;

and her mother, Hélène, cared for the littlest Lalanne, Baptiste.

Whenever she could, Marguerite would sneak into the fairground
to see the rope dancers, jugglers, and acrobats practice.
How she missed the circus!

At home, she begged her parents to let her learn to ropewalk.

But they forbade it.

What could a nine-year-old girl who longed to dance across the sky do?

Marguerite staged her own *petite* revolution.

She sought secret lessons from Monsieur Barraut, an old family friend and leader of a troupe of acrobats, Les Sauteurs Patriotes.

Soon Barraut posted public notices throughout town,
announcing a show featuring a remarkable young rope dancer,
Mademoiselle Ninette.

The Lalannes were eager to see this talented new acrobat.

On the evening of the performance, they joined the gathering crowd.

Dressed in a costume decorated with ribbons of red, white, and blue—
the colors of the revolution—
a small girl leapt onto a rope.
She jumped,
she twirled,
she danced the gavotte and the minuet!
Mademoiselle Ninette was a wonder.
Mademoiselle Ninette was . . .

MARGUERITE!

Her mother fainted.

Marguerite's papa rushed to catch his child.

But Marguerite did not fall.

The audience clapped and cheered and called for more.

Inspired by Marguerite's passion,
her parents decided to leave their ordinary life behind
and return to performing.

They assembled a traveling circus troupe that included

a juggler, a conjurer, and a ventriloquist.

Her father directed the shows.

Marguerite and her mother starred as rope dancers.

While the Lalannes roamed far and wide,

lifting the spirits of people struggling with hunger

and the hardships of the revolution,

the king fell from power.

So did the queen.

And finally, so did the government.

But the Lalannes did not fall.

They danced on.

At the age of eighteen, Marguerite married Julien Saqui, an acrobat.

She joined her husband's small family circus,
performing as Madame Saqui.
But Marguerite longed for more—
higher ropes, larger crowds, bolder costumes. . . .

She longed to return to Paris!

In 1806, she visited Les Jardins de Tivoli,
a spectacle of fireworks and flowers,
waterfalls and lanterns,
and best of all,
aeronauts and acrobats.

There, she watched the Great Forioso

walk across a tightrope—

and fall,
breaking his ankle.

The next night, Madame Saqui took his place,
waltzing and pirouetting on a rope
stretched high above an admiring crowd.

A few months later, she sashayed across the river Seine.

And a few years later, to celebrate the birth of the emperor's son,

she skipped between the towers of Notre Dame.

Napoleon was the new ruler of France,

and Madame Saqui was the darling of Paris.

As Napoleon waged war across Europe,
Madame Saqui reenacted his battles.
Napoleon gave her the title
Première Acrobate de Sa Majesté l'Empereur et Roi—
First Acrobat of His Majesty the Emperor and King.

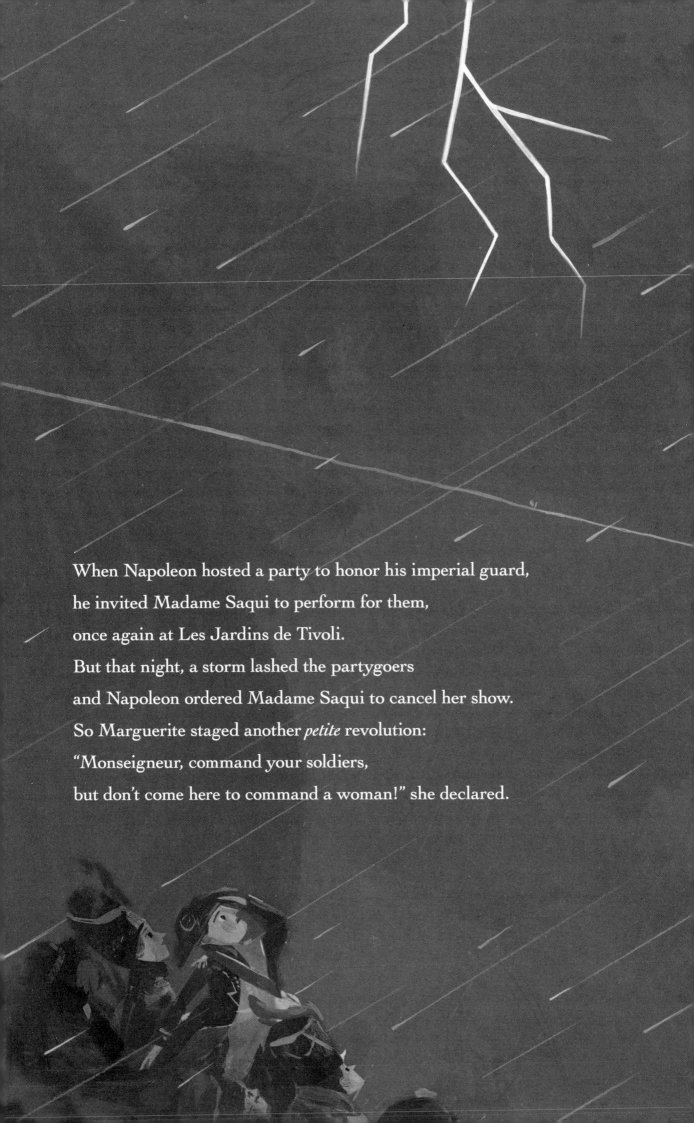

When Napoleon hosted a party to honor his imperial guard,
he invited Madame Saqui to perform for them,
once again at Les Jardins de Tivoli.
But that night, a storm lashed the partygoers
and Napoleon ordered Madame Saqui to cancel her show.
So Marguerite staged another *petite* revolution:
"Monseigneur, command your soldiers,
but don't come here to command a woman!" she declared.

She darted onto the rope.
And as the rain poured
and the wind roared,
Madame Saqui soared high above the crowd.

For many years to come,
and in spite of many hardships—

the death of her husband, Julien,

the loss of her theater, Le Spectacle Acrobate de Madame Saqui,

and the theft of her life savings—
Madame Saqui danced on.

When she was sixty, Marguerite announced
that she would walk across the tightrope
just one last time.

Yet after that performance,
she could not stay away.
As the days, weeks, and years passed,
she returned to dance across the sky,
again and again and again,
well into her seventies.
It was her *dernière* revolution.
Madame Saqui simply could not say farewell.

And she never fell.

AUTHOR'S NOTE

Madame Saqui pursued her passion for rope dancing at a time when society imposed many constraints on women. Although women have practiced this perilous art for hundreds of years, most famous wire walkers are men, such as Charles Blondin, who crossed Niagara Falls on a wire, and Philippe Petit, who walked between New York's Twin Towers. Madame Saqui achieved international fame before these men were born. Her story adds a woman to the cast of characters on the stage of circus history.

When Marguerite-Antoinette Lalanne was born in 1786, revolution was in the air. The American Revolution, which had ended in 1783, inspired French citizens to call for social and political change. Marguerite's childhood took place against the backdrop of the French Revolution: the storming of the Bastille prison in 1789; the fall of the monarchy in 1792; the beheadings of King Louis XVI and Queen Marie-Antoinette in 1793; and finally, Napoleon's seizure of power in 1799.

Although Marguerite was not a revolutionary, her conduct was. Her scandalous costumes outraged and delighted audiences. Parisian women imitated her style, wearing ostrich-feathered hats *à la Saqui*. At Vauxhall Gardens, her flesh-colored leggings created such a stir that she had to change into pantaloons to perform. Women were not supposed to own property in the 1800s, but in 1816, Marguerite bought a theater and named it Le Spectacle Acrobate de Madame Saqui.

She faced many setbacks: a cholera epidemic that drove Parisians away from theaters; the exile of her patron, Napoleon; and the deaths of two sons. Nevertheless, she persevered, rope dancing through two more waves of revolution in 1830 and 1848.

Her story inspired me to try wire walking. I practiced on a low tightrope in my home. But you don't have to own a tightrope in order to learn. Most large cities have gyms that teach circus arts. Beginners start on low wires with a mat underneath. Why not give it a try?

GLOSSARY OF FRENCH TERMS

dernière (feminine form of dernier): Last. Madame Saqui had trouble deciding which was her last performance.

gavotte (also English): A lively dance with skipping steps, popular in eighteenth-century France.

Les Jardins de Tivoli: The Tivoli Gardens, one of the earliest French amusement parks, featuring entertainment such as concerts, fireworks, and magic lantern shows (early slide shows).

Madame Saqui: Mrs. Saqui, Marguerite Lalanne's married name and her stage name.

Mademoiselle Ninette: Miss Ninette, Marguerite's stage name for her first public rope dance.

minuet (also English): A slow ballroom dance favored in Louis XIV's court in the 1660s.

Monseigneur (also English): My lord, the title Madame Saqui used to address Napoleon.

petite (also English): Small. Madame Saqui's revolution may have been small, but she lived a large life!

Première Acrobate de Sa Majesté l'Empereur et Roi: First Acrobat of His Majesty the Emperor and King, the title Napoleon gave to Madame Saqui.

Les Sauteurs Patriotes: The Patriotic Jumpers, a troupe of acrobats who wore the tricolor (red, white, and blue) ribbons of the revolution and performed at the fairground in Tours.

Le Spectacle Acrobate de Madame Saqui: The Acrobat Show of Madame Saqui, the name Madame Saqui gave to the theater she bought in 1816.

Le Théâtre des Grands Danseurs du Roi: The Theater of the King's Great Dancers, the Parisian theater where Marguerite's parents performed when she was five. During the French Revolution, the theater changed its name to le Théâtre de la Gaîté—the Theater of Gaiety.

BIBLIOGRAPHY

Blondin Memorial Trust. "Funambulus—A Potted History." blondinmemorialtrust.com/funambulus.

Coke, David, and Alan Borg. *Vauxhall Gardens: A History.* New Haven: Yale University Press, 2011.

Cook, Eliza. *Eliza Cook's Journal.* Vol. 7–8, 254–255. London: J. O. Clarke, 1852. Accessed online.

Ginisty, Paul. *Memoires d'une Danseuse de Corde.* Paris: Librairie Charpentier et Fasquelle, 1907.

Leroux-Cesbron, M. C. "Deux Danseuses." In *Bulletin de la Commission municipale historique et artistique de Neuilly-sur-Seine 7–9* (1910): 68. Accessed online.

Leslie, Frank. "Madame Saqui." *Frank Leslie's Ladies Magazine* 10 (1862): 145. Accessed online.

"Rope Dancing." *Pall Mall Budget* 24 (1880): 12. Accessed online.

Schama, Simon. *Citizens: A Chronicle of the French Revolution.* New York: Alfred A. Knopf, 1991.

Stanton, Sarah, and Martin Banham. *Cambridge Paperback Guide to Theater.* Melbourne: Cambridge University Press, 1996.

Telegraph. "Famous High-Wire Acts Over the Ages." telegraph.co.uk/film/the-walk/famous_high_wire_acts.

Wall, Duncan. *The Ordinary Acrobat: A Journey into the Wondrous World of Circus, Past and Present.* New York: Penguin Random House, 2013.